Google Classroom:

99 Ideas how to use Google Classroom effectively. The Ultimate Guide to Learn Google Classroom.

ISBN: 9781796520453

CONTENTS

Thank you for purchasing this book!

We always try to give more value then you expect. That's why we've updated the content and you can get it for FREE. You can get the digital version for free because you bought the print version.

The book is under the match program from Amazon. You can find how to do this using next URL: https://www.amazon.com/gp/digital/ep-landing-page

I hope it will be useful for you.

Introduction

Have you heard about Google Classroom?

It's a new learning system that can really help you create a great learning environment for students and teachers. However, some students are afraid to use this and some teachers are against using technology.

Well, it is time to dispel some of the issues that you may have with this.

This book will go over the tons of features Google Classroom has to offer, and some key aspects that will ultimately help with your ability to use this. If you have ever been curious about this, well you are in luck, because this book will tell you all about Google Classroom, and the features.

Here, we will discuss over 99 different features that Google Classroom has to offer, and some of the key aspects of Google Classroom, why they matter, and how to utilize these. We even will throw in thirty ways to use tests and assignments in your classroom to help you better understand this amazing system!

By the end of this, you will be looking at Google Classroom and will totally understand why it is an important one, and why you should always consider adding this to your repertoire of different items to try out in your classroom. Whether you're a new teacher looking for something new to use with your students, or a teacher who has been in the business for a while and might be hesitant upon using this system, everyone can benefit from this if you use this system, and ultimately, you'll be able to create the best and most worthwhile system that is out there, and that is offered.

You can use Google Classroom to you advantage in many different classroom environments, and you will learn from here why it is one of the best ways to engage your students, and why it matters.

Chapter 1 – What is Google Classroom?

The first thing you might ask is well, what is Google Classroom. We will discuss here in this chapter what Google Classroom is, and some of the new upgrades that were recently done to Google Classroom so that you can better understand the different aspects of Google Classroom.

What is it?

Google Classroom is a web service that was developed by Google for educators and schools with the purpose of making assignments paperless and to streamline the file sharing system between students and teachers. Essentially, this uses the entire Google ecosystem, such as Google docs, slides and sheets for writing and presentation, the Gmail communication system, and for scheduling, you use Google calendar. Students can join the classes their teachers have made with the use of a private code, or are automatically imported from the domain. Every single class is separated based on folders within the drive, students can put work in there, and teachers can grade it. It essentially is like putting your entire classroom on a computer, and it does help streamline both the education, and the communication between the teachers, and the students alike.

The coolest part about this, is that if you don't want to talk on a computer or use a computer, there are mobile apps for both Android and Apple devices that lets students do assignments on their device, even put photos on there, share different apps and files, and also access information on their devices both online and offline. Even with this, teachers can contact and speak to students, they can monitor how a student is doing, and once they are graded, teachers can go back and add comments to their work on order to ensure that students have the best education possible.

Essentially, this has made teaching way more productive, it also allows teachers to manage the coursework that is there, and everything is in one place, providing a more meaningful collaboration between both of these parties, and ensuring that students get the help that they need when the going gets tough.

The system actually allows more administrative tasks to be done in an effective manner. Because of the G suite for education, it makes tasks that are otherwise boring much faster. It works wherever you are, teacher or student, whether it be from any computer, any mobile device, or whatever, and it allows teachers to have access to the assignments that are there, the course materials they need, and all of the feedback in one awesome place.

The coolest part about this is that it is free. It's free for schools that have signed up for G suite for education, and like with any of the tools the classroom meets one of the highest standards that's out there, and ti's a super fun system, and it is free, and works better than most free software that's out there.

Another great thing about this, is that I t allows feedback to come back to the student right away. Educators are able to track the progress of a student, and let them know how they are doing. More focus can be put on making sure that the student gets it, which is something that many students want to have. The cool thing about this is how integrative this is to the workplace for students, and teachers will be able to help in a much timelier manner. Plus, it allows for a more personalized construction, and it will allow students to have a better time learning subjects as well.

For teachers and students, it will save them time, effort, paper, and it will allow teachers to create a better environment for assignments and quizzes, and you can always talk to parent s and guardians with this. You can copy and tweak assignments as well one to another, and control multiple classes as well, which is great if you are looking to truly master this type of system. It is great for students and teachers alike, and allows for a collaborative system that will in turn create a better and more immersive system than you have thought possible.

Many praise Google drive because of the accessibility of the devices, the utilization of Google drive, and the ability to go paperless. But, it does have the disadvantage of little support for external services, although that's changing, the lack of auto quizzes, and also the lack of any live chatting that teachers can use for feedback, but it's obvious that Google is looking to update, so we may get to see these changes sooner than ever.

What are the New updates?

There are always new updates happening, and as a teacher or student, it is important to consider these updates. You actually are going to get some new and immersive updates to classroom that can ultimately help you.

One of the newest updates actually just came out in December of 2018 and that is the Classroom Gradebook. Which is a beta, but if you as a teacher want to edit and look at grades, share them with the students, or even create weighted grades and calculations on either a mobile or desktop version, you'll be able to fix the grades on the fly. You'll need to utilize the beta and sign up for this, but there is a lot of support that's available for this.

With this, you can use the tool that helps with trading, and this can be used with videos, various PDFs, and also the documents that you need. You can also put the assignments together by modules and units. You can use this to engage with students so you can give the students feedback on their items, and what can be improved upon, allowing for more engagement.

You can also determine where the documents come from. For example, it can be used with google docs, but you can also use it for other documents as well in order to help improve feedback to students.

There is also a new update that allows you to turn of specific notifications. Therefore, if you are sick of your phone going off in the middle of class, this update allows you to eliminate that, and makes it easier for you as well, and you will be able to create a better, more immersive learning environment. Google Classroom wants teachers to continue to talk to their students, and to facilitate discussion, so that everyone gets heard and there is a bigger student voice, and even share the readings and reference materials, allowing for it to get bigger and better than ever before for every student.

The stream has also been put together in a much better manner. It's always been there, but usually, the announcements, questions, and assignments are all there, and now, with a new update, it keeps the announcements, the posts from students, and the replies there, making it a discussion stream, so that the assignments, and the questions you may have are all moved towards the classwork page instead.

Then there is the people page. In the past, you'd go to the students page to message students and guardians, and the teaches would be in the about page, but now, if you want to see everyone, whether they be teachers, co-teachers, guardians, or students, you can now do it all under the people tab, which is right next to the classwork page. You can email, remove, and for students mute or for teachers make them a class owner, which affects what they can do for the class.

There is also the student selector, which is great if you want to call on students that you want to have discuss something. This is a feature on android, and from this, teachers can choose a random student, especially in the case of answering. While students may not enjoy this, this new feature allows for more participation, and if you do not want to think too much on who to choose for what, this is a way to facilitate that. Finally, let's discuss the new settings page. In the past, all of the functions were in different locations, but, the new settings page all puts it in a gear that is located near the top right location whenever you go to the class. Essentially, when you go to the menu, you choose that, and you are given many different options. In this, you can choose the class details, which you can use a pencil in order to edit and change, and you can even change the location, the description, or even where classes meet. You also can get the class code here, which allows you to give this to the students if they have to self-enroll within the class. You also can control what students do on the stream page here, whether they are allowed to post, place comments only, or it is just a place for teachers to do announcements. You can also control whatever gets deleted here, which is good if you notice when someone posts comments or posts that aren't appropriate for the class or even for school. Finally, you can find out the information from the parents here, and the guardian summaries that can ultimately be changed if you feel like you need to add more information. It has a separate settings area that teachers can look at and consult, in order to help facilitate the use. It also allows you to have a less cluttered about page and in turn will allow for more resources to be used in the future. It does create a great difference, and ultimately, is something that allows for some great changes to Google Classroom.

The Google Classroom is a great addition to any school, and if you have been confused as to what it can totally do, you can read all about it in the ensuing chapters. Nevertheless, the purpose of this chapter is to give you an idea of what Google Classroom is, so that you are not confused anymore, and in turn, can understand it even better than before.

Chapter 2 – How to Create Quizzes and Assignments in Google Classroom

You can create assignments and do a lot with both this, and quizzes in Google Classroom. Here, we will discuss some features involved with creating assignments in this.

1) You can create an assignment by signing in, choosing your class, and then pressing the plus button, and creating an assignment.

2) You can change the assignment details by putting in the description, and changing the due date.

3) You can choose whether an assignment is graded or ungraded by choosing the option as well.

4) You can also add materials to an assignment by going to upload for files, and you can also choose by pressing the down arrow whether students can view, edit, or if you want to make a copy for every student.

5) For YouTube videos, you want to click the YouTube option, search for it, type in the keywords, and then click on the one to add. You can also attach URLs to by entering the URL and choosing to add.

6) There is an option to recreate the assignment again by choosing the link and clicking on this.

7) The create option allows students to create file sand drawings right in classroom. They just press create and then make the assignment.

8) If you want to turn in the assignment, you just press turn-in when a student goes to the assignment.

9) If you want to create an assignment on android, what you do is tap classroom, choose the class, and then the plus button to enter the assignment. From there, do the same as before.

10) If you want to change the due date of an assignment, you go to due date, choose a different date or time, and then press done to complete this.

11) If you need to make announcements to the class, you can choose "create announcements" in order to make these.

12) You can always, with every single Google Classroom tool you use, create a link and attach to it by going to link, and then choosing to share the link with it.

13) You can use it for both turning in items in drive, and also for documents not available in drive

14) You can create quizzes by choosing quizzes, and then choose to make it a quiz.

15) However, you can choose whether or not the students see the results, or if they are held on so you can grade it individually, and you can choose whether students will see missed questions.

16) If you want to set it up so that it self-grades, you can create multiple choice answers, and then press answer key, and you put in the answer. The self-grading option only works on multiple-choice questions though.

17) You can also do this in Google form by creating a form, choosing accepting responses, and creating one page for answer keys, and one for the questions.

18) You can only use this for an exact match situation though, so do not expect to rely on it that much.

19) You should make sure that each of these have names on them, so that the student has an option to fill out the name, and in turn, allow for the student to have a better ability to say what the answers are

20) If you want to create assignments related to spreadsheets, you can create a survey with this. But, it doesn't have a "skip logic" function like other software

21) Teachers can use Google forms as well for surveys and other student assignments and even add or edit different questions you want students to answer.

22) Forms can also predict the teacher's answers, which allows "smart" quizzes to be used and saves teachers time.

23) The predictive text can also help you add some trickier options and curveballs, and will do so automatically

24) You can also choose what students see after a quiz by opening the quiz, going to settings, choosing quizzes, and what the person can see, you check what you want to show.

25) You can also under quizzes, go to general, and then under the "requires sign in" uncheck that it is restricted. This is good for students that are not in the system jest.

26) If you don't need to attach assignments, you literally just have to press to mark the assignment as done, and it'll be seen

27) With Google Classroom, you can always attach various items, whether they be forms, or whatever, and if the document has your name on it, you can turn it in by opening and reviewing the document, entering further information, and then turn it in. The teacher will automatically see this.

28) You can attach other items by, when you are turning in an assignment, you press the down arrow and choose the link to attach it to, and then turn in so you can confirm this.

29) For assignments that just need to be marked done, you can always click the assignment and leave private comments. All assignments are in the class calendar too. Unless stated otherwise, you can always unclick an assignment as done, choose to edit it, and from there turn it in to reconfirm. Obviously if it is past the due date, you will not be able to do this.

30) One feature Google Classroom has that might be a problem, is that if you turn in an assignment again, it'll be marked late. Teachers will have to manually go in and fix that.

31) All assignments can be edited by choosing the option and then choosing to edit it. You can also choose to add comments by going to view the assignment, hit instructions, then add class comment and post.

32) To undo assignments, you go to classwork, choose the three dots for more, and then choose to delete. You can delete once again to confirm this.

These features allow you to utilize Google Classroom and the assignments that you want to add. It is simple, and very effective.

Chapter 3 – Google Classroom Apps and Features

Here are some features of Google Classroom along with Apps that you can use and enjoy.

Add Materials

The best thing about Google Classroom is you can attach to these various videos, surveys, PDFs, and other items that you can utilize from Google drive. Students can, with this draw on, write down notes, and even highlight various elements with the PDFs within the classroom app to make it easier.

Customize the Class Color

Class themes and colors is something that you can integrate into classroom. You can, with this, go to the settings, and then choose the default color or a theme for your class. This does help if you are working with multiple classes and want to make sure you provide the information to the correct class.

Assignment calendar

The assignment calendar has the purpose of keeping both students and teachers better organized. Each time a teacher creates something within Google Classroom, with a date on it, you will have it immediately on the class calendar. It is easily found by going to the three lines on the left corner area of your screen, and from there choosing calendar. Once displayed, you can see all of the work that has been assigned, whether you are a teacher assigning work to a class, or a student getting work from the teacher.

New Work Area

The new work area within Google Classroom does have assignments that are outstanding within one place. If a teacher does not grade an assignment yet, it will be there, which is good for students who are curious about whether or not something was graded. In the same vein, if a student has not turned in something yet, it will also show up there, so it is good for teachers to find out what they need to grade and good for students who need to figure out what it is that they need to finish up.

Communication with others

Communication with parents and students alike is something that Google Classroom does decently, despite the lack of a live feature. The students can put posts to the stream of the classroom, which in many cases can be a good discussion board, and it is good if you do not want to have the question answered right away, or it is to a dire need. Many times, if you need to contact the teacher directly, there is a means to email them, and teachers can do the same. The stream is moderated by teachers as well, and you can attach media to each of these. Gmail also allows for students and teachers to communicate on the interface. Moreover, with the introduction of the classroom apps, it allows for more integration on there as well.

Archive courses

You can also archive courses with this. With Google Classroom, at the end of a semester or year, you can choose the course, go to settings and from there, and archive it. It is removed from the main homepage, but it is not permanently deleted, so teachers can look at the current year and look for any assignments they want to keep. You can view it, but you cannot make changes. Deleting a class completely gets rid of it in its entirety, and many teachers decide not to do that, especially if they have assignments they enjoyed from the previous semester.

Organizing Stream

You can utilize topics in order to better organize streams Every time an announcement is created, teachers can assign the topic to the category for every post, and let it be organized. Whenever it is created, the topic will be on the left-hand side of the stream, and when it is selected, the topic will show up. This allows teachers to put together content within the course, so you can organize the class into different units. This is great for history or biology teachers, who tend to need different units for everything they go over.

Share to Classroom

The share to classroom extension is available for teachers that use either laptops or chrome books within the classroom, and this extension allows teachers to show the screens and work within the class, so teachers can share websites to the computer, and they can essentially click on the extension, and from there choose to push to teacher. Once finished, the teacher is notified that they will show the screen, and from there, teachers can essentially do the same thing by showing students their screen. You don't need to have to show a screen anymore, since it's all there.

Activity Learn

This is an app that works super well with Google Classroom. It is good not just for languages, but also for English, social studies, and even biology. This one works well with Google Classroom, and you can even jigsaw, take the entire class, and even closely read some of the different aspects. Teachers can use this app if they want to bring some great and integrative activities to the classroom. Moreover, all of the assignments do synchronize back to Google Classroom.

Aladdin

This is more of an app for teachers than it is for students themselves, but Google Classroom fully integrates with Aladdin. That way, teachers can plan the roll, create grades and also put together reports too. Teachers can also find information in a super quick manner, meaning that they can find out the date the student enrolled, their parent, the class, or the staff information, along with any relevant documents in a singular lace. The rolebook also will even be integrated with other apps that allow for alerts to be given in an absence, especially if they're in other classes, any trends of students, and also, to help reward the attendance of a student so that they feel better, and it allows for a more integrative system of learning for students and teachers alike.

GoGuardian

This is a great tool not just for teachers, but administrators, and even counselors too. You can filter the settings for students, get less few false positives, and even allow for better classroom management with the assisted tools, and with geolocation enabled on this, it allows for any devices that are lost or stolen the chance to recover. This is great for using the laptops in school as well. For teachers, it also allows students to show you what they are doing in real time, create an activity timeline, and some scenes, which essentially allows for better working places, and less distraction. With GoGuardian, you can integrate this with Google Classroom in order to ensure that students are creating a better environment for themselves, and teachers are less distracted as a result too.

Little Sis for Classroom

You can use this in order to create rosters that are integrative, and allow teachers to archive the classes not needed, and allow for better and more efficient organization for teachers, and to make it more efficient for teachers as well.

There is a classroom explorer, which allows one to have insight on the classroom adoption, and allows for administrative actions on the classes too, and with the sync jobs function, it will maintain everything in one place. It also has a more centralized guardian system, so in places where you need to have everything all put together, you can look at the current state of the guardian invites, and from there, send guardian invites to students. It is run manually initially, but it actually goes full automaton once it is started, and it is really nice if you run lots of classes, and need a good app for that.

One Click Worksheets

With every worksheet, you can create individual documents for every single one of them with a singular click. This a nice feature that saves you time so you don't need to copy everything to every single student since that can get quite annoying.

Class Resource Page

One awesome feature of Google Classroom is the fact that you can always create a class resource page for any documents that you need to utilize with your class, including the rules and the syllabus. To do this, is first to go to the classwork page, and from there, you choose settings, and then choose to add class materials with a title on there, which will help organize the class a little bit better. You can always add multiple different resources under a singular title, and then add them with different names each time. You ca then choose to attach and then choose the icon that is relevant. You can from there, choose the item you want to add, and then add either upload or add. To put a link on there, you can always click on that or add a link, and you can always press X to remove the attachment, and then press the option to post. If you have it in each section, it allows students to go to it at any time, which is ideal if they need to review the syllabus once again.

Exporting Grades

You can always export the grades you have to Google sheets or to a CSV file to see all the grades at once. You can only do it on the computer version, so you can't on mobile. To do this, you click on your class, go to classwork, the assignment, and then choose to view it. You want to go to student work and then press the gear icon and from there, you will want to copy all the grades to Google sheets, and then, you will be able to see the spreadsheet in the drive folders.

If you want to export the grades to a CSV file, you essentially do the same thing, and you can choose whether you want to download the specific grades as CSV, or if you want to download all of the assignment grades as a CSV, and they'll be in the downloads folder so you can externally import this.

Creating Individual Assignments

Google Classroom also allows teachers to create individual assignments, and in turn, this allows students to have a personal assignment if they need it, which is good if there is a chance that they need to do something specific, and this also can be used for announcements as well. It is quite nice, and you will realize when you use this that it is easy to implement, and simple to organize your assignments with.

Alma

This is another student information system, but it is the first to do the job of fully integrating with Google Classroom. Throughout the integration, teachers can utilize this to synchronize the grades and assignments, and it can also be used with teach teams in order to manage everything across the districts and the schools that are in the vicinity, which allows for better organization. It's nice, because it will showcase the different trends, and allow one to see what is happening, which is great if you're looking to ensure that you've kept up with everything in the school.

CK-12

This is a very handy app for students that features over 5000 different spelling, science, and math concepts along with lessons, and students can access tis content wherever they are. If your students need some extra resources to learn a subject, this is one of the best ways to do it. Students can learn at the pace that is comfy with them, track their own personal progress on the subjects, and from there, even work on assignments and get deadline notices, and even recommendation for learning resources they can utilize, and a lot more. It covers everything from basic concepts to even geometry and biology and calculus, and it is a major resource that will work for different educational levels.

Curiosity by Beacon Solutions

This is an app that allows students to have all the knowledge that they want easily, and it's one of the best apps for Google Classroom. Curiosity is one that is perfect for those students who do not want to stop learning, and you can learn a ton through using this. There are 5000 different articles and a million different videos on any topic imaginable, so you can use this with practically every grade level out there, and no matter the subject.

Whether your'e using this to understand science, or better utilize this for history and other subjects, the videos and the articles that are there will tell others about the subjects, and in turn create items in a rewarding and beneficial manner.

Discovery Education

This is an app that gives digital media, textbooks, curricular resources, and videos for so many different subjects. Most of the major disciplines, including math and science are available here. It is a great streaming resource too, and it even contains modules, personalized instructions, and guidelines that will help. It's more than just a streaming source though, but it also has interactive features that help with assignments, including skill builders, audio clips, and even activities and assessments. It allows expending in the classroom more from a more static to engaging sorts of experiences for yourself.

Uncheck

This is a great option for Google Classroom in that it offers a great paper similarity scanning resource for students and teachers, in order to eliminate plagiarism in the classroom. If you are a teacher who does have assignments that involve research, use this in order to check the assignments to make sure everything is original, and not stolen from anywhere. If you are a student, it is good to use this, since it will prove your authorship in the future if there is any potential issue and you need to defend it. So what makes it different from other plagiarism checking? Well, it has different functions specifically for educators, in that the checker will recognize any reference sand citations, which are common in most papers that are written, and it allows for it to work in real time in order to check various databases, and it is one of the best for integration into Google Classroom.

Duolingo

For language students and teachers, this is the app for you. It can be hard to learn languages, and for teachers, it can also be quite frustrating, but Duolingo is one of the best apps out there, and it involves a lot of activities to help those learn languages. It's got 23 language options to offer, from Spanish to French to even Japanese, so you can learn the language by using this app. The lessons are small, and you can even record yourself talking to see what it sounds like, and to help with pronunciations. It is quite nice, and it will even let you have conversations with bots. It's one of the best apps for those who are looking to learn languages, and it's free to download.

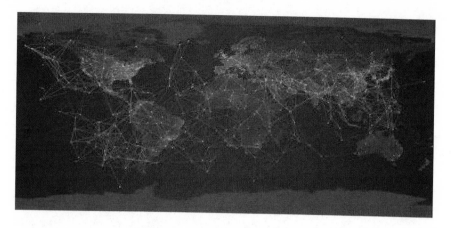

Quizzes

This isn't just any old quiz making app for teachers to use, but it actually makes the quizzes easy to understand, are educational games, and it allows for you to assign homework and content related to it. It is in the form of a quiz game that makes it fun for students and teachers and the like. What teachers do is they create a quiz using one of the pre-made ones, and then they assign it. While they play, the teachers control the timer and leaderboard, allowing for it to show any knowledge gaps that need to be honed, and anything worth working on for everyone. It's a great quiz system that is perfect for review time with students if needed.

Padlet

Finally we have Padlet, which is perfect for art students in that it gives them digital canvases to create amazing projects they can share with others. Students can also collaborate on the app, and they can work to put a lot of this together. It is one of the coolest and most rewarding apps currently on the classroom, so many teachers like this for partner projects, not just for art students. This is also good for if you want students to collaborate and work together on simple assignments, in that it's got videos, interviews, the ability to upload documents, and even writing out texts and theme customization. You can create discussion boards, Venn diagrams, or even business plans for business students. This is an app that allows you to do so much, and it is a fun one for students and teachers alike!

With some of these integrations, you will be able to utilize the apps that are such easily, and create an interactive learning environment that you and others will enjoy. Google Classroom has so much to offer, and so any different elements that teachers and students alike will enjoy this, since it offers a lot for them to utilize, and different aspects of this as well.

Chapter 4 – How to Communicate with Parents Using Google Classroom

Communicating with parents and guardians is one of the key highlights of Google Classroom. However, how is it done? Well, you are about to find out. Here, we will dive further into how parents can benefit from this with teachers through the communication with parents and guardians,

Sending Announcements

One of the key ways to communicate with students in an effective manner, and you can also send these to parents as well by pressing the settings option and being able to communicate to parents. Teachers can use this as a discussion option, or even share helpful resources for students to benefit from, which is great if you want to utilize this for parents to work with.

However, teachers can also be kept in the loop and one of the key things to consider is trying to communicate with parents and guardians through email summaries. These are something you can email to the parents, and giving them a chance to opt in for that. The emails are used to help parents understand what students are doing, as well as any announcements on future work that may happen in the future. Parents want to be kept in the loop when it comes to the future of their children, so this is one of the best ways to do so.

Parent notifications

Now, if you have parents that are super worried about their children's activities, you can enable parent notifications. This is similar to what was said before, but what you do, is you got to the students area, and then choose to invite the guardians next to the names of the students. From there, any email address their parents or guardians have will be put there. From there, the parents can get any summaries of class activity, and this will also include missing work that students may be dealing with, and parents can choose whether they want to get daily or weekly summaries. Many times, weekly should suffice, but if the student tends to have issues, then maybe a daily summary might be good for the time being.

Once the email is linked however, do make sure that you realize that parents and guardians will have it fully available to anyone in the district or domain, which may be why some people do not want that. You can also opt out of this by going to the "include the class" option and choosing to switch it off if you do not want to have that on.

Google Form Parent Teacher Conferences

With the advent of new technology and Google Classroom, one thing that has changed are parent teacher conferences.

Google forms can be done to make copies, and from there, you'll send this to others, and from the copies, you can send these to the parents and guardians. From there, they can choose when they want to come in to see the teacher for a conference.

If you've ever had to deal with choosing when a guardian will come in to the classroom, this is a good way to fix that. The form is simple, you just put the name and contact info, and from there, you can choose the time. It also prevents loss of the papers and such when a parent gets a simple email and the chance to choose the time that is best fit.

The coolest part, is that this is linked to your google calendar, so you don't have to worry about forgetting the meeting or anything, which makes it easier for parents.

But, if you want to do this on a form alone, you can always send out the form to the email addresses, and every time you get a response, you put this in an excel sheet, and you can read through, look at the different aspects, and figure out what you should discuss with the families. This is a great way to figure out how to run parent teacher conferences., since you won't have to worry about the awkward conversations that you may have otherwise with the families.

From here, you as a teacher can set up the intervals, based on what times work for the families, and many times, you can do these conferences. Faster if you do have, a form that's discussed what parents want to focus on and any issues with the child. It does streamline this, and many times, it does create a difference since it will help students meet the goals, and parents will be more engaged. It allows for you as a teacher to address the concerns directly with the students and the parents, and creates a bit of an n idea of how to prepare. But, the one downside to this is it may require a lot of preparation ahead of time, but not much more than what it would take otherwise.

Communicating with parents is quite important, in that it ca help them better understand what is going on, and in turn create a better, more integrative atmosphere. It is a different way to teach, and teachers actually end up getting more parent participation than ever before. If you want parents involved, this is ultimately the way to do it, since they will be more informed of what is happening with their kid, and be able to change anything as needed, or talk to the kid whenever they need to.

Chapter 5 – Correcting Assignments using Google Classroom

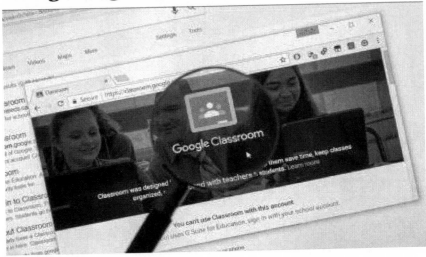

Grading assignments is quite easy in Google Classroom, and while we did go over quizzes, let's talk how to grade individual assignments in this, and some cool tips with this.

Grading in classroom

Grading in classroom is quite easy. First thing you do is you go to the classes that you have and check out the assignments tab. From there, you can see who has and who hasn't completed it, and you can then click the number over those who have finished to showcase who has finished the assignment and turned it in. From there, you can click the name of the student to see the document, and then look at any documents attached to it. You can from there read it, grade it, and then close it and then go to the student work page. You want to click on the person who had the assignment, and it will say no grade. From there, you type in the point system, then press the check box, and then choose return. Once returned, they are recorded, and classroom will ask if you want to attach any further feedback. You can choose what to do there at your own discretion.

Setting Points

One cool thing about this, is that you can choose how many points an assignment is now in Google classroom, which makes it much easier for grading. You can put the tally of points at the top now as you add or edit questions. This is done automatically, and it's part of a new update and machine learning. So, gone are the days of trying to calculate how many points something is or how many questions, you can set it yourself., and Google will do the work for you, saving you lots of time.

Shared Doc is Best Way

If you are looking to quickly get feedback to the students quicker, always make a Google doc for shared assignments, since that does provide quicker feedback when grading them. You can always choose to "add comments" and from there, add comments and feedback without changing the document within classroom itself. You do not have to mark up pages in red anymore, but if you want to, you can still use red ink for correcting them, which is really nice. If a document is unfinished, and the student is asking you to give them a bit of feedback, you can go into these right away and see for yourself. What needs to be changed. In a similar vein, if you do use a Google form template for the skills and homework points, you can always change these as well, and if it's changed in a similar way, it allows for a teacher to quickly give feedback to students.

Shorthand Grading

You can actually use symbols and abbreviations to grade these, and if you set these in a correct manner, the document will change these. You don't have to worry so much about writing down countless amounts of information, but instead, you can type in something as simple as "sp" and through machine learning, Google Classroom can change that and insert in there "spelling issues/wrongly spelled" without you having to type out so much. It looks better, and students will understand what you mean by that.

Auto Grade Questions

If you use grid style questions or checkbox assignments, you can create the correct answers, and the quizzes will be auto graded, and it creates an easier system for teachers so that teachers don't have to ask the same types of questions, and instead collects everything in a way that's smart, and effective as well.

Decimal Grades

How awesome would it be to give partial credit on something in a simple, yet flexible manner? Well, now you can with your Google forms, and a recent update allows you to give decimal answers. For example, if the answer is half-right or maybe they are missing a part, you can now give half of a point, and that will allow for more exact grading. You do not have to write a copious amount of notes saying where some student was half-right, and what went wrong. It allows for much more exact grading, which is super nice.

YouTube Feedback

Some students learn better if they are given a video to better understand a concept. Instead of just trying to write it out twenty times in hopes they will understand, why not give a YouTube link to the issue they are struggling with. This is a super awesome means of helping students understand a concept that they don't totally grasp whenever you grade it. You can pair it with a link either to YouTube, WatchKnowLearn, Khan Academy, or other educational resources, which is perfect if a student is struggling with a concept, and needs that little extra boost to help them understand the concept in a better manner.

Doctopus and GeoRubric

These are two really helpful apps for grading. Doctopus is an add-on to Google sheets, and it is a teacher created tool that allows for managing, assessing, and organizing projects within Google drive. It essentially begins with a starter template that's mass copied, and from there shared. The same template can be used to manage the grades. Goobric is an instrument that can help create an efficient grading rubric for the student's grades, and will help with seeing as well just what the grades of a student are currently. By pairing this with Doctopus, you essentially will auto fill out a rubric, and from there, Doctopus puts it onto a spreadsheet. It saves you a buttload of time trying to grade everything, and these two apps are both integrated with Google Classroom, which in turn will allow teachers to do a whole lot more with this, and allow for a much more integrative and better learning system.

Grading assignments is a teacher's job, and while it may not be the most fun job out there, Google Classroom has made it way easier, and simpler. With some of the new additions to this, it allows teachers to create a system that allows you to have a simple, yet effective sort of job that they will enjoy. When a teacher uses this, they will realize just how simple it is to integrate this into the classroom, and from there, they can facilitate grading, and get the feedback that students want on their work. It creates a better, easier system, and it also gets teachers much more involved in their student's progress since they can keep track of what needs to be worked on, and what students are grasping easily.

Chapter 6 – Advantages of Google Classroom

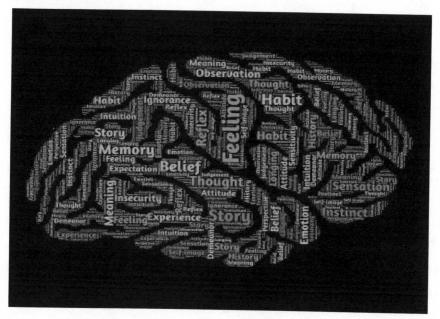

So what is so great about Google Classroom for both teachers and students? Well, read on to find out. Google Classroom is great for both educators, and for students, and it ultimately does make it easier for teachers to do their job. Some teachers may be against the technological changes, but there are many benefits to this.

Better Accessibility

Google Classroom can be accessed from any device that uses Google chrome, regardless of platform. This means, you can work on your assignments on an iPad, or even on a mobile phone, and they're uploaded to Google drive and the classroom folder, meaning they can be used wherever, whenever, and students never have to worry about losing their assignments anymore, that's for sure!

Saves Paper!

Google Classroom is completely paperless, so you won't have to worry about printing thirty-plus copies for students that have a knack for losing their papers, nor do you have to worry about students misplacing paper well, it's all online. All of the assignments are uploaded there, and once there, they're saved to the drive, which means that students can complete the assignments there, send it, and it's saved to drive, and even if they don't save it, it's there so you never have to worry about students using the "my computer crashed" excuse for the third time.

Exposes both Teachers and Students to Online Learning

Since it's all online, Google Classroom allows for students to work in an online environment, which is something that students will soon learn about the moment they go to college. If you want a master's degree in education, you need to actually do some of your work online. The same goes for many majors, but many students don't know how to navigate an online class. Well, Google Classroom is a great way to actually understand how to work in an online environment, and by being exposed to it early on, it allows for them to not be as shell-shocked when they finally make their way to college and realize that they'll have a lot of classes similar to this in the future.

Super easy to Get Materials

It's also super easy to access the materials, but this is good because no matter where they end up, they'll get the materials. Students that are absent can get the classroom materials from home if needed by simply logging in and getting the assignments by clicking on this. Gone are the days of having to deal with students having to chase after you just to get assignments.

All Work is There

One thing that's super annoying and frustrating for teachers is the fact that some students have a knack for losing work. Well, Google Classroom nips that in the bud. How? Well, it takes out that external document, and instead everyone works in Google drive. Google drive saves everything immediately, regardless of if you make one change to add a word, or if you work on the assignment for hours on end. It's super nice, and it saves you a lot of headaches. It's all there, and students never have to worry about "accidentally" losing work.

Creates Collaborative Learning

Because everything is digitally, you can share content with peers in one singular document that can be edited together, and then share another version for the students without the editing to this. If you want to, you can create assignment worksheets that are different for teachers and students, and from there, drive together a question and answer system, and even create deeper discussions. It allows for teachers to really engage with students. With the way technology is bringing everyone together, it's no wonder why teachers want to integrate this further and further into the classroom.

Instant Feedback and Analysis

Gone are the days of having to wait for whether or not you did well on a quiz, or if you will get enough answers. Teachers don't have to sit around and meticulously spend a ton of time grading assignments. Instead, you can deliver quizzes that have automatic answers, or even give a detailed report on what teachers can do better. You can help those who answered questions incorrectly add more to this, which is super nice, and it is super easy to integrate into the system. Students will get their answers faster, and teachers can grade everything in a more detailed way.

Saves you a Ton of Time

For students, this saves them a ton of time trying to save various documents, hoping that it gets to their drive, or even just working on paper and awkwardly turning it in. It also saves them time on answering questions, because let's be honest, a day could go by and they may not get the answer right away. By utilizing Google

Classroom, you can save yourself. a boatload of time, and ultimately participate way more in this as well.

Communication Success!

This ties into the previous point, but Google Classroom saves you a ton of time when it comes to communicating. If a student has a question, they can send an email, comment on an assignment stream, send comments privately, or even provide feedback on something. Teachers can do the same, and the teachers can as well send specific emails to communicate with students that have a specific issue, or who need a lot more help. That way, they won't fall behind. It is making a difference in terms of how students handle the workload, and teachers can also follow the different standards, and in truth, it makes it so much easier for everyone.

Students Take Ownership

One thing that teachers try to help students get better at, is trying to stay more engaged in their studies. Well, Google Classroom can help with this. It is not just students reading and commenting on answers that the other students may have, it is also being in charge of their homework. Students can learn a subject they're having trouble with a little bit better if they are struggling with it, and in turn, if they want to utilize additional resources on their won, they can. The best part of Google Classroom is really just hos students can take charge of their learning environment, and in turn, create the best learning experience that they can.

In-Depth Data Analysis

If you want to see whether or not students understand, and any areas they may be stumbling on, this is how.

You can even take the grades and export them from google sheets, or just keep everything there. If you want to analyze and sort them as well, in order to see how students are faring and where you need to focus, you can use this as a super helpful resource tool.

Lots of times, you can see trends in grades, and if you notice there is something wrong with a student's learning, you can take the information that's there, and from there, use this to help students get a better idea of what is going on.

Teachers can get more involved with the use of google classroom, and they can see just where their students need some help, and any other resources that can assist them as well to be successful.

Good Security

Security is actually very strong on this. If you have an IT team, they can control the passwords so if a student does forget, they can fix it quickly. With the API that is there, everything is synched up, so the teachers can have everything put together. It's also got a high-level security, which means that you won't have to worry about any breaches and the like, for it's also quite easy to work with.

See that Real-Time Progress

Are you sick of trying to have to walk around and see whether students are working on this, or maybe you want to help students if they are going in the wrong direction? Well, now you can with this. With the Google Classroom system, you can press Student Work, and you can look at the thumbnail of every single student in order to see their progress in real-time, so you can track and see if there are any problems if you are looking to change this. You can also use the revision history feature to look at changes that have happened, allowing you to see what worked, or what didn't work, and how you can fix that.

See All the Work

Finally, with a new update, you can look at the student's work. This is great if you know that a student is missing an assignment, and they are claiming they turned it in.

Teachers can do anything from making conferences to even meetings and study groups with google classroom through the use of their system. You can also look at all of the work that a student has put in, meticulously choosing different ways to help students benefit from their studies and other resources too.

Everyone can benefit from this, and this chapter highlighted just what Google Classroom can do for teachers and students to help facilitate learning even more throughout the semester.

Conclusion

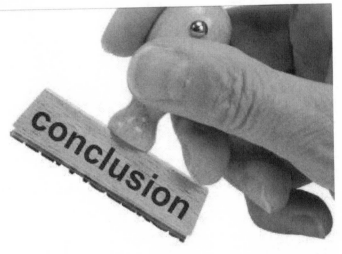

Some say technology is going too fast, and some people may be against the utilization of technology, but let's be honest, with the introduction of Google Classroom, it allows for teachers to work with students on a more personalized basis, and in turn, you'll be able to in essence, create a better and more rewarding learning environment. You'll see for yourself just what this can do for you, and why this is one of the best systems out there for teachers and students to use together. It might be a bit confusing initially, especially if you're not used to technology, but if you're thinking about bringing your classroom into the future. This is ultimately the way to go, and if you're a student who is about to learn how to use it, you'll see for yourself that this is a simple, and very effective means to truly create a great amount of engagement with your students, and to make it so that your students will enjoy the process of learning.

Learning is something that can be made fun, and with Google Classroom, you can achieve that and so much more.

Your next step is to work with Google Classroom. Play around with it, and make it so that you know how to use the system, whether you're a teacher, student, or a parent.

Through understanding what you're using, you can create a conducive learning environment that works for everyone, and teachers will soon notice that students are better with this, they'll be more involved, and parents can keep an eye on anything that's going wrong, which creates a better classroom, and a more beneficial learning experience for everyone, and it does change the game by a lot as well for everyone.

I hope, that you really enjoyed reading my book.

Thanks for buying the book anyway!

Made in the USA
Lexington, KY
27 March 2019